THE NEW FREQUENCY

&

The Music of Annihilation

Tod Thilleman

Ma'arri

Princeton

Cover art: Kenneth Bernard

ISBN 0 - 9661242 - 0 - 0

Ma 'arri
156 John Street
Princeton, NJ 08542

ma-arri@rocketmail.com

http://www.freeyellow.com/members/ma-arri

Library of Congress Cataloging-in-Publication Data

[Thilleman, Tod]
        The New Frequency; & The Music of Annihilation/Tod Thilleman
                p. cm.
        ISBN 0 - 9661242 - 0 - 0
        I. Thilleman, Tod; New Frequency   II. Title.
        III. Title; Music of Annihilation
PS3570.H453N49   1998
811'.54--dc21   98-4791
                                                                    CIP

The New Frequency

for Charles Borkhuis
who said the courage needed
must mine

Recursive hell of man's
Cyborg the dæmon-led
The beastial

   Æon of identification

   We
   One

Toward becoming but else

In germ-resistance-coupling-heat. . . . .

From out the shores of the island of the world
My home-spun cruel edict
Where age has concentrated
Spoken for the coming
        And, in so
Culpable stance
Spit straight
Configuring chaos
Gas from the belly of bloat
Signals
To sight
        For transistorized fragmentations
Density of a timid age
Amor gentle syntax
        Mimicking wave-length
Whose might
Theos broke

Where
                        are the times of difference fallen. . . . .

The spiritual is but the dust of ignorance
And the mind its arbiter
Reckoning from dull flint
Of outmoded sunlight

Or it is the re-composing of suns within detritus
Mined by fire's jealousy
Realized by the sensory mannequins of identification
Intensified in a moment of oblivion
When the clock struck
Pulling all
With it

Or it is only one cauldron
Retching forth the blind eye that heals
Until tomorrow's reason bans all knowledge
And hangs
From the idle and alarumed

Collision of empirical cells
Multiplying over the face of the earth

Ecstasy flutters

Sending to the eyes
                    and mind

Recording device dendritic
Cavity of spring-time

Sounding out green treaties
True intellection the planet the species the coded genetic
Scientific category-breaker
Cataract of authority. . . . .

What connected sign of a barrier they weep. . . . .

We must now hue toward sanctity
Of nothing
Squaring no geometry

       In the coming day

Spatial immensity the chemically coded universal structure
Joking laughing in the hollows of man's fate already arrived
Forcing sluice of cellular homeostasis

I know men and women beyond
Under the terrible next
Whose terror has told the magnificence of being
And whose creation has signaled the might of no world

For we are a barren life
Wed to the manacle salvation
And have no enterprise in the starry depths of infinite space

Mortal sacrifice allotted human enterprise
Sucked into girders of a solid radio-relay station of the name

Entertained to certain death

The aged pretend a wizened vacuity
Static in the memory of a once-vitalic
Now but the pharaohs of crude hoax and bastardization
From the womb of women to the cloned inception of death
Spreading beyond bounds of allottment the beatific unearthed fruition
Procreation of industry

Banishing morally dense texts
Enslaving population
Forever
The human will dies
Terrorized to the categories

Come to the furnace for the resurrection of the grave
Dæmon-like, wandering, fulfilled in destiny

No formula

     For in the lowly creeping
Advance of age
Images lust
And break their seed
Abandoning Being all Being once fled

We to take hold in raiments of an æon's light
Wrap out the dim flagging specter of death and decay
In inverse polymathed equation
A like epithermal propinquity

We have the technology the mean-density ratio to amor

Position integrity an eidolon
Deep the frustration
Meat against bone

Wearing deep badges of certainty out of ages unknown and known

In the time of the coming of the belly's epoch

Spread your liquid in the uneasy fire of remembrance

Now that the
That even them who have died
Pass this way again
Gone to the finitude mankind was in the name of infinity

Figures of death. . . . .

Driven into sources of history from a Fatherless race
Propped alignment with space

Forward
For emolument of all past living specters
Vain gods of a dendritic earth
A circularity
Over vaulted heavens
Within calling walls of a leveled
Interstitial animation

       Radiant waves conduct the pulse
Concerted effort bears. . . . . .

   History now not
The charter of temporary sanity
But the chartered

Presence damned

Whose time indeed rises within the infernal depths. . . . . . .

    Into the rising emanations
My own made contraption
From scraps of what is

Down to the intellection of the humming atomic capacities

Whose arms and legs have sight
For song in space
Down to the drilling drive in the air
In stations of mankind's perdition

    These too the notes
Industrious begetting
And in whose cataracted fall
Toward gathering
And the philosophic rendition
The dæmon's birth-form
Dissolving metaphysic
Thus elevating sight under sign
And in semblance to levitational anti-gravity
Our world takes to beginnings of a new epoch.

Singing hollow meaness
For the searching flight
In bonds
For the animation

Wings that in the dæmon's new charge the low are lifted
Toward what heights no mage know. . . . .

      Fulfilling prophetic category
Perpetrating hoax
Circle within the squared
For the winning of that epoch
In terms of an æon's ape. . . . .

Wed-lock to secure
And not the productive
Reasoning deadens the dead-pan maneauver upright
Toward discharge
Of duty long held
In the mind of most

Cries out from beginning of the end

The box rattles
Shakes the capacity of a blind urge
Outgrowth of word
For flight of its dark wings
Over lines of a telegraphic eternity

Toward atmosphere of æther
For the re-capacitation
Harbored
Visited
Rising to meet its antithesis
Mined
Inverting
Blowing glottal density
Progressing eyes
Telling thru world domination atmospheric pressures
De-stabilizing
For engagement
From out the time of the crumbling of nations

Burning durance in the capital of rude coinage. . . . .

    Industrious mirage
The heart-rate of the new world. . . . .

    For now the earth has come
Whereby fallen seed released
Revives thruout
From its universal relative
Radiation
Thence on it seems

Again and again
Striving to undo us
Our own signaling commands
The sound from Okeanos

Levels now out
My own capacity. . . . . .

    The walls
Just beyond the life-leak
The misery of history the usurping touch has blinded. . . .

    All the coming
In the veins of my hands
Between accumulating knowledge
Between the planes of a geometric
Within the capacities of air
These are the futures
Spelling wonder
Silent
Hung up
Capturing vain epic.

Breath of the denizen of tomorrow
In the faces
In vanquished
Unleashed
Whispered
Sweeping

Coming up for air in the æther of the picture
Trailing in dust

Released thru the agency of sex
In recursive organs of animals

Come to the forest
Bedlam in the folds
Sent on the blood

There in the hollow dendritic
Cavity of earth

Blinding darkness in the anthropomorphic
Helixed thru darkness
Caught
Flung
Separated
Commanded
Aeons have goaded

And the machine
Captivating life-times
Sucked self-hatred
Nowhere
To be itself

Sailing in interstitial moment of eternity
Pronouncing it on lips and tongue to the helmet's capacity
In the dendritic time of man
In the vain little

Come

Denied the caterwauling precincts of contingent categories

All the rooms just off
Held in reason
Pronounced on the tongue......travelled thru space.......dead in the earth.. . . . .

      Dark eye of the bird of the moment
Clinging
Whistling
In the time of the
In the time of a

      Practiced in the heart of the living exhumed
Captured
Rocking me
Saddled
Flown
Pushing forming moving containing its making
In the time of the falling of nations. . . . .

Between the walls of the characterization. . . . . . .

In the hallway of the century......behind the eyes of vain glitter....
In the practiced positions
Thru the blinding furious assault of a wingéd dæmon. . . . .

Captivating trestles
Mirroring
Over cities over earth over worlds far below . . . .

How themes give way to strong winds
Into
Focused
Visionary and threatening
There to enable
Static in the firm push

Masking the totalitarian. . . . .

    The chemical the earthly
Hung by infrastructure
Blasted by the cortical response of sensorium

Moving into
Usurping
Pursing for the kiss
Of universal structure. . . . .

    The dead hours and years
Vain amorphous
The cancellation of a moment
For the overthrow
Tuned to the mechanical
Emanations flee

From the historical base of an abandoned empirical
In the research facility of the will of industry
Within the buzzing reflex unanswered
In the density of a nothing a brain the size of nothing
Rocks the dendritic capacity
Vain dynamic
Tied to tubes of liquid signal
All for the positive logical advance in the hollows of
For the primitive reflex
For the helixed maneauver
Sexual and universal from the sparking genitalia
Usurping in quantum mechanic of rumor
Thru rocket tubes of a scientific will
For the distribution of system beyond the stars.........
Toward capitalization of bone-marrow
Adhering lips to the might of the mountains of what is
Strong singing capacities from the dark of man's enterprise
Deep layered formation of a chemical whim
Whose chart sent war in search of itself
Toward the core problematic in the shape of Earth
Mankind grabs with a hand the individual has not seen
Computes the intestinal of the great distribution
For the ability of the monster ethos.

The New Frequency's enduring return..............

Sent by hands and feet.......flow of distribution along identification.......
The burning durance of nothing

Research facility
Within markets of industrial cost-cutting

Steps the progressive movement toward intensification
Within time of the falling of nations

My youth down the drain of identification
Out under the faucet of empirical dynamic research

Incisors the test-operative channel frequented

Focus of the body in preterite somatic realizations
Terminal nodes
Research capital
Hook up in heat.......squeemish......names ......

Time is the capital of order
And anti-body's defending vain center of neo-awareness
Struggling toward density that is the order of all I am
Within matrix of
Within æon of the host of logic and the images of amor

Within womb captive solitary confinement
Practiced in the playground of the mind

Breath from the goddess
Circulating
Center

Capital in the purple *stimmung* of the philosophical
Spat on the wishful presence all presence now becomes

Circle the dense matter from the root of primordial time
The local atom-smasher
The spiritual dynamo
Length now the body of the ego in historical transition

Focus the epithermal agencies
No one left.....æons of involving humanity.....mothers of the dead.......

Factories of the infamous agencies
Beacons before the blast
Death the enzyme empirical force

Research divulging rumor
Beast harnessed
Soil hermetic signal chasing vision

Character of fiction.....composition.......flinging dendritic atom-smasher
Fist-fucking eternal program for historical imperatives.....chandeliers.....
Spreading the world onto grids of the signal.....deadening the hard-on...
Faces of languæ-lexical programming densely driven empirical tower......

Belief the transmitter
People the lost eidolon
Sight the expositor
Words emotive digitalis of epoch........

      The one into many
The spatial density
All has been given to the backside

Capacity of the lumen erected by her interests

What exists. . . . .

She burns
Un-real kingdoms
Delivering epoch to æon

History forms the young in gestative tube
Daemonic incunabula flesh out the machine.....
.............data primitive....Jesus Christ......

Slipstream to become the modus operative of cities......over.......

           Fund the unconscious
Character driven into

Every identificant a penetration of the signal
Failure operative they feed upon.......centrifugal atomizer.......

Release the sperm for the communal button......dæmonic urges ....over....

Slavery transubstantiates.....chemical codes conceal....twentieth century...

Rising figures of futural density in the moist womb of history
Replicate machine's desire in a coded enzymatic relay station...................

Schizophrenia questioner to write a cultural consubstantiality...........

Spittle forming in the sides the cheeks.......no-man's land......sight.....

      I am the soul of the death of labor's energy
Condemned to the incunabula of historical spirit
Holding allegorical consubstantial anagogy
Without effort
Without learning
We are the people
We are the soul that wanders...........
We are the unwanted in the mouth of epoch...............
Animal that beasts about our body........

Bursts of signal in the retina
She is the soul's oblivion
My history fades into pavement the city's secreting
Funding feeds the research......one face to face.................
....gravitation......universal sorrow.....

These are the signals......ancient shells of nacreous neon....................
Interrupted by need in the channel...................................they cover the ground so
fully...
.....................................what?..

Save yourself from the matrix....................................nothing attacks from an errant
nothing.......................................

Eye-balls carry the burthen......................fantasy conjures the sky..... ....rev-
olution breathes......................

Who?

The ripple forgets the water....cyborg calling....will and words in lurch
....

      Beyond which we are
Within sight and tone of her within time and space
Now the heart's deluged by the turning tide of epoch
Toward body of desire in folds of dumb scientific behavior
Toward spark
Funded from above
Making live the germ in reproductive capacities
Supreme weight we have died to unending night
Within the strength of hand and feet and thigh
We have perished
Tidal exhaustive anti-human wave
Dead to the spirit of eternity
Curving thruout
Empirical dynamics of a theme-park..
....
....
....
                        ....
                 ....

The Music of Annihilation

The construction of a basic set of twelve tones derives from the intention to postpone the repetition of every tone as long as possible.

—Arnold Schoenberg

The theme portrayed the hard winds of mind
When occurrence of dust amplifies that occasion
Mining done and the harried and lonely town
Looks into itself for connexion's next similitude
Unburdened by the name it singularly chose
Hidden within time like the particles entrancing rude shape
Whose night belongs in trash with the rest
Emanating vast riches in rumored moments
Sprung from sounds of this hissing storm
Roaring out rashly from a hunk of the world's wood •
Thus were we betrayed in the world's woodpath •
Music cries from the lighted cinders of our love
Announcing death's musical tribute solitude
Surrounded memory
Of a western rush •

Now is the entrancing moment made supine
Wondered by the tentacles of history's past and present future
Laid there by the sweat of one form both beautiful
And ugly to the core of its essential extension •
It laughs out toward the space of the world's omens
And trudges half-life toward the door of light •
You are the falling might of my own sight
Made useless reason in the pillows of lonely thrusting
Nerves that ordered the world from beginning to end
Pangs of heartache that serve our master sleep and the void
Must now arrive, severed and barely discernible
Yet bloody and carnate within dream I most admire •
Tonight, when humans can no longer stand to live
You will guise the distancing machinery
And oblique our travail
With thought •

How time keeps our rounded timing straight
Thus can we see toward the blighted structures
Named Energy by the social physicists of our wake
Yet un-named by the pure sound of time un-interrupted famine
Whose peopled immensity warns of size without variety
Yet whose peopled expanse cannot comply its own
And so we lust toward heart and mind as foreign body
Ending marriage of far-flung enterprise and mirth
For joy un-covered swiftly moving intelligences
Rattling in the sound of the world, battling against mind
Un-hinging the properties of conscience
Opening toward the real death of course
And seem-sewing whatever flesh might signal
Thus encapsulating life by its own tail
And giving to birth's lineage
The smile forgotten in personal sorrow •

That the individual can throw off what it is
And regard what is not, in a nameless place
Secures the dark and deadly musics of our day
And, forced to discern, it will level all it loved
Calling the four winds as it loses late its eyes and mind
Worldly bereft and cleaving to the scheming rumors
There to foothold its fallen life-duty •
We are the product of no principle of thought
Yet the will strives toward both the seen and invisible
As if our nature had want of neither
And so the moments come and go
Or linger in the mouth of every God's creation •
Outside my arms they still pursue their dreams
And tho I craven image in the like of intelligence
And string my bow's strings tight over any character
Mankind but has one bark and bite
One mother, one father, one fate to blame •

No way out unless it has no sound
The terrible breathing deathly music holds
Structure at bay within temporality of mind
Whose traps are laid by the door to space
Whose will engenders the future of a frozen race •
They want lite nothing to invade the planet
Usurping cellular lust, boring the sound-soul
Raping silence with the belief of non-existent God
And, thru force, subdue particularizing relation •
I am alone because I love you •
Technical directives lead to hell and away from you
And yet, believe these drives that mask the wind itself
Come closer to the source, closer to the real
Come closer to all knowledge
Terrible and great •

You own the same as I
And yet its opposition is written
In non-empirical dynamics of the chemical nature
And all the world rejoices at our touch
This simple expression bridging the mirror with kisses
And rumoring political and religious sentiment of the world
Into its non-existent face and mind and handless rage •
We never meant the annihilation those oppositions mean
And bless their existence in our coupling strange
Spelling out the distance of the entire universe
Within song of one Being born toward the end •
What path could there be but this
Sonorous and lighted by nothing but what is
Thus painfully becoming itself out there
Beyond mankind's reasonable sanctions
His heedless exhaustion expanding
Death's resolve in the depths of silence •

Death's music saved me •
The world lives in my belly and brain •
The edge of reasonable themes transgress with my self
Whose open composition takes the name
Delivering dispersion of its intelligence
On the dead engines humming vocabularies too far aloft •
The human animal cannot confront
The animal that lives in the breast of existence
And so flounders in intellectual haphazard wind
As if it were what it can never be •
The blunt night saves me
Where I read the dizzy portions of its rest
And have finality for my kind-continuing time
Whose limbs swallowed the vault of heaven
In earthly punctured sky straight above •

I am the unspoken matter of the world
And face the wonder of my cage
With expert alertness of a nymph
Dropping down to the shallow bath of her lake •
The sound of theme had music when I turned
And thrust me up toward the mistaken brain of art •
It sits at the bottom of the empty staff
And fills each space with notes of mortal value •
There was never any ground but that of time
Which winds about the growing substance
From which we take our names and number
From which we take our fame •
The enlarging field of tones and pathetic deliberation
Entrance the bird, the rose-bud
And write with gestures of authority
Harnessing the will of man •

There never was anything within the mind of man •
Access to the idea of whole symphonic worlds
Now bristles with the law, with identificants
Whose ears are coiled within their own spanning universities •
Come forth child of the world from the womb of story
Thus succumbing our rooms to re-construction
In the name of head-sucking benighted belief
And the self-hood that lives in its grip
For mine are the kingdom of familiar type
In never-wandering neo-fabulation of seeming folk •
From here to the moon reflecting sun's light
The system rings in the simple system's sayings
Phrases, repeated, and rendered by delayed mind's flow
Which desire exemplifies as this age •
I wanted to paint your place in the world
But found my role-assigned fate •

Now wind is everywhere the call of mind
And sex the only foundation reviewing it
Thus are my scars held within all gashes and wounds •
I would set behind the stones of indifference
And push them toward any goal space projects
Thus bringing me to the feet of the mountain
Where the hermit lay awake feeding on nothing but sight •
His Being spent among rock and the dense realities
Abhores my tongue and the picked up resonance
Shored within •
I am your ambassador, take me as yourself was taken •
His skin recedes to the endless distances of Being
From which my veins flood with terror and pride
And share the human lot alone •
I own the faculties death performs
And music my existence between event and event •

Love discovers music not thru program
But thru self gone over, out, and above
Thus ending tyranny within the mind
Thus envisioning a new world in a piece of distance •
I feel the coming extension of all places within my body !
Everything has been given to the deepest waiting
Accorded in releasing enzymatic systems
For the confluence of eternal progressions
Now landing in the very soil of matter •
Thematic recompense now wanders the world
And feeds upon the grasses of love's shade
Copulating in the multitudinous æons of sound
Gathering the artistic and empirical dynamo of mortality to a head •
In distance, what alien echo repeats my inner vow •

Accomplished : thematic role death has with music
Set down in words the man emerges
His chance arrival in the row he most furrows and hoes •
They have set the air on fire with electrical disturbances
Set the soul apart from its mistress
Covered her with the speech of a mind that lies
Torn love from the world and set it down in the ground of pain •
I am the trespassing sound of inconsequence
Made in the belly of God, routed out by inconsequence
Whistling thru the winds of the memory of nothing
Warring with the human in the shade of existence
For the winning of dust in the town without pity
Drowning in uncontrollable environments the weather sends •
Hang them in the yard where the eye-beam lingers
Sentence them to the force sound joins
In musical representation this moment uncovers •

Why should words represent the creation ?
Our focus comes from eyes and mind and the beard
Long and shaggy on the face of composition •
What place moves but the death-like place of life itself
Whose maneauvers have told the time deep into fascinating niches •
I knew not what continued but now I approach
And find the life-body frozen once again
And from the dim mind the population of judgement springs
And loads ignorance with the station of my own soul •
Moving in the underground I became the train
Manufactured of a thousand years of knowledge
But not one could penetrate you today
And no message sent down the halls of any abode
Would worship your tender dying wail
In the new light of this or any century
Or spate of time come undone with talking
Or with the brain of language •
You have slipped into the essence of the void
And seek the knowing way as if it were on wings
Given by the wind of time itself
Given to be itself the element of creation itself
Inaudible at the edge of volcanic chimes and mercy
Leveling the receptors with the ears of re-arrival •

Cage saw music trapped by the word of God
Manacled in the teeth of reason
Extrapolating the essence of proportion
Into vain gullies of deaf relation •
How can touch know the whole flow
Unless that flow knew itself only as touch ?
My knowledge knows no moment
But places as it was placed
In the center of centeredness •
Things come and go •
What drives the existence
Drove the existence to re-write
As it had done at the beginning
Whether by its own hand or another's •
My closely contested breath wants to smash
All the dead icons of your lap
And swim within the fable of a hunter
Of the hunter and the hunted •
Now let go !

My words know the reason of Being
And music-mimic in the light of the sun
Or the wind or the elemental candence of a rock
Or hollow cave whose darkness swallows all •
They all received pink slips
They all hunkered in the hive's walls •
In error, let the composition have power
To sweep them from this spot
For this is the interior of the poem
And it sucks at the depth of depth itself •
What is it that is this large world
Made up of intimation and of shallow chips of salt ?
I want it to think but it is
Dead •

I have a pain where consciousness should be
Closing down the rounds of the deserted towns
Showing them the value of a full tone or stop •
Thus was the world made to breathe like you
And thus were we sent to the end of time itself
Searching for nothing, laden with nothing
Burdened by the poem as if it were only an exteriority
As if all living things were externally procreative
Disposing our identity to nothing but the fire
The wind and the elements composing our constitutions
Our future gone into some other worldly relation
Here-to-fore un-harnessed and un-kept
Here-to-fore at-one-time abandoned
Now re-considered and working against all language
Against everything but privacy itself
For the last shred of evidence of self
With which to measure the vastness of space
And the intelligence inherent in a piece of matter •

Belief walked and talked like anyone, like me •
The energy of the planet possesses music
Not just the sound the sound of the dead
Where they speak in the street and meet •
I was brought together by the absolute mercy of existence
Which knows no mercy
Which no doubt knows nothing •
She has opened her thighs to such music
As would make me rush toward death •
They think music leads to the sound of the dead •
The drift of continents signals for me to beware
Existence has claws that mangle •
To seek the deepest repose following on the heels of useless knowledge
She evades and the storm clouds resume their patience •
What person I was or am is nothing compared to my person
Teleo-lodged in the world of Being •
How much can I swallow before I become ?
Is the mind the relation to all event
Tumbling in upon itself ?
Am I naked ?

All simple personable relation and reason
Has now bloated and this is the mark of the age •
I know that I know nothing •
You will never realize how profound those thoughts are
Nor as things happened how they will happen again
Transposing the real upon a populace and skinning them alive
For the sake of a material possession
Whistling thru æons of obsession
Was there any true need for us to proliferate ?
She comes at us with her teeth bared from jealousy
All meaning extracted from that terrible vengeance
And the meek inherit the earth's dwindling resource
Un-touched for so long
Hindered by nothing so much as Being •
I wish to stay away from you
In order to enjoy your final coming within thematic design •

All my speech touches upon music and fails within itself
Grasping for the horny thought of the time of the coming of music
And despairs in my occupation of it
And the multitudes within it
Rasping toward nothing for no one
Exists but this trembling nerve-dance of the intellect
Stored within thematic repose like memory •
I'm the man I always thought I'd become
Severing logical catenation in the charms of one single head •
Was it only a character within heard the call of the wild
And threw its arms around my throat
Pushing me back onto the bed of hearing and logic
Unzipping my maturing fly ?
Buzz goes the beetle, and snap goes the bug
I am drawing nearer the planes of attraction
Where the rumps of the world lift to be sniffed
Spoiling the epoch's fascination with mystery and love
Sex and the garden of one earthly fall •
I worked to possess music unknowingly
And now press my attention in the name of it •

I think I thought and still think I am
When the deadest theme of all lurks as the ground lurks
And makes music as the world •
And yet the outside persists to attract the ego
And murder the mind for its continuation in existence
Such is wisdom ill prepared and a meager salary for hire
And such are the words of the body made into dynamite •
Was thought the only way to make music ?
I have seen all people in kindly and mean plaint
Rest themselves on the beast of all nations
And blow out the network with their desire •
She has been made definitely a temporary fixture
To be thusly manipulated by hands more firm, stolid
And controlled by planetary force •
I lusted after perfect spheres of my own making
But the cognition of existence indeed resides outside the cogito •

No way to get back to the center the interior
Without first realizing dismissal of music
Oops I almost said language •
She rallies around the image evoked by the listening •
Won't anybody try annihilate this love
Sending us to the upright historical position
Or must we sweat and slut
In a fascination with disease and inconsequence
Till death do us part •
We have been released from all obligation
Because everything shows for the central theme
And clusters about the heart of Being
Resolute in the self-image of the absolute •
I thought my Being would exist forever
But it knows only hiccups in the music of a moment
And thus have I sought to plant the single digit of creation
Within creation's very lap
And let linger its possibilities a little longer
For the new epoch •

What is forming within the conceit of a womb
Pulls at all diction from the void of its brainy purpose
Vain and pompous from the center of existence •
We are the Salitter voiding worlds into bowls
Flushing out the material thought as if it were a language
Sprung from the brow of authority's dark and sinister purpose
Conjugating its fly-snap on the waters of the world's river
Enticing fish to breed in its ripple-wave of memory
All place retains no matter the forgetting human maneauver •
Time brings the music of delight that forces the chattering birds to flee •
Are the extensions of space the relations of my physical mind
Blurred by the real and set up inside the real for that blur
For purposes beyond the fascination of the enemy ?
Have I made a world as THE world ?
How small the people seem
Within any scheme •
If I am mad then it was not from the word
That spoke to me from the flight of music
Whose wind witnesses the true powers of the seed •

Idiot mankind, those that are
Not dead within the annihilating bosom of dream
Wed themselves to the vacuum of all possibility
And concept the transept of virginal pride
Within grade and curve the world seeks
Thus have we been betrayed by white dawn
Thus have we been shaped and carved and umbilically hewed
From massive sides of the sky of blood
Whose beasts reside in the mouth of non-extrapolating essence
Embryonic to the end, stupid and blind as force itself
Naming the intellect of human kind in the thought of force
Handed down by the fixtures of hallways
Rude and uncontrollable by reason's new-found delight
Blackening this time this mindful age with every conceit
The machinery musters
Usurping instantaneously the might of my only Entelechy
For the sleep-continuance of thematic voids
And dim unrealizable gigantisms within the tiny fate of fleas •
Earth's wind now rests as the secret foundation to man's power
Battling the intellectual foes of Being and the foes of darkness
Each a sketch in eternal progression of the other's mask
The absolute having failed to arrive once again •
My belly seeks to understand the attraction of that fountain
Pumping out crystalline seduction
In the cognitive fury of my restlessly counter-rising ego •

Stopped dead in our tracks by any thing that appears •
I thought the infinite to be a part of existence •
We arrive at the center of theme as we arrive at the center of the poem
And burst forth every held nothing into a storehouse of nothing
Expanding its useless wealth for all to see
Expanding the structure of the knowledge of creation
Expanding to stand in the reason the body makes
Expanding toward the fantastic light the brain has erred
Succumbing once again to its projections and finite wind
Yet finding in the whole a use for the energy atomically gathering
Souls for the clarion push of horny sound and light
And the map of this place we have created by lowering our self into •
Self seems to have always been the phenomenon of eye-sight •

All music might now be embedded in this set
And unitized as mind-theme and death-extension
Thru-out the realms of planetary music •
What stops and starts, march and become
Now tell, thru thematic precision
The lowering from aloft of every scale
Into one, tipped and flowing toward Being in excelsis
Wherever the material of the world
Coalesces impossible Earth of ultimate value
Truth honor and the host of tiny man in rightful repose beneath it •
Born for the restless energy and continuance of existence
The mind's vain chatter and storehouse of apprehension
Bows and enters the way given by time and space
Thralled in the dialectical triumph of music
Whose art no one knows
But whose practice within desiring winds of mortality
Begins and begins again against the walls of tissue
The orders of its place •

Tod Thilleman is Editor of *Poetry New York* and the author of *Wave-Run* and *The Corybantes* (Spuyten Duyvil).

Kenneth Bernard has taught for many years at Long Island University in Brooklyn. The author of dozens of avant-garde plays, Bernard's theater work has been performed mainly in collaboration with John Vaccaro's Play-House of the Ridiculous and with The Living Theater. Along with being a collage artist, he is the author of *Baboon In The Nightclub*, and *How We Danced While we Burned* (Asylum Arts) *Clown At Wall* (Confrontation Press) and the novel *From the District File (Fiction Collective)*.